The Kid's Book of
Simple Everyday
Science

Kelly Doudna

SCARLETTA KIDS

MINNEAPOLIS, MINNESOTA

The Lexile Framework for Reading®
Lexile Measure® 700L
LEXILE®, LEXILE FRAMEWORK®, LEXILE ANALYZER® and the LEXILE® logo are trademarks of MetaMetrics, Inc., and are registered in the United States and abroad. The trademarks and names of other companies and products mentioned herein are the property of their respective owners. Copyright © 2011 MetaMetrics, Inc. All rights reserved.

Library of Congress Cataloging-in-Publication Data

Doudna, Kelly, 1963-
 The kid's book of simple everyday science / By Kelly Doudna. -- 1st ed.
      p. cm.
 Includes index.
 Summary: "These simple science activities will have young kids searching the house for everyday items to learn about temperature, pressure, water, air, heat, and plants! Each easy and fun activity includes how-to photos, simple instructions, short explanations, and introduces beginning math principles. With tips and extra information to extend the scientific experience, this book will get kids thinking like scientists in no time at all! Book includes: supply & tool lists, visual and text-based explanations, step-by-step instructions and photos, and safety information."-- Provided by publisher.
 Audience: 5-9.
 Audience: K to grade 3.
 ISBN 978-1-938063-34-3 (pbk. : alk. paper) -- ISBN 978-1-938063-35-0 (electronic : alk. paper)
 1. Science--Miscellanea--Juvenile literature. 2. Science--Experiments--Juvenile literature. 3. Science projects--Juvenile literature. I. Title. II. Title: Simple everyday science.
 Q163.D685 2013
 507.8--dc23
                                    2013010372

Book design by Mighty Media Inc., Minneapolis, MN

Publicity: Desiree Bussiere, desiree@scarlettapress.com

The following manufacturers/names appearing in this book are trademarks: Alka-Selzer®, Arm & Hammer®, Barq's®, Coca-Cola®, Dawn®, Diet Coke®, Gedney®, Heinz®, Ivory®, McCormick®, Morton®, Orville Redenbacher's®, Pyrex®, Salon Series™, Schweppes®, Sunkist®, Up & Up™, Welches®, Wesson®

Printed and Manufactured in the United States

Distributed by Publishers Group West

10 9 8 7 6 5 4 3 2

Contents

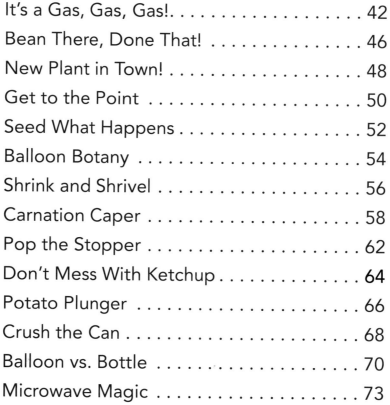

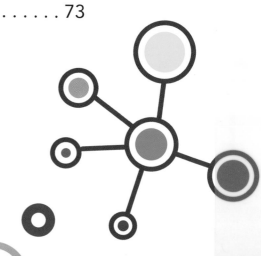

Super Simple Science

Do you want to be a scientist? You can do it. This book will help you. All great scientists started out where you are now. They began by observing the world and asking questions.

Science is in everything around you. It is in bubbles and balloons. It is in plants, potatoes, and popcorn. Do you know why an index card can seal water inside a bottle? Do you know why mixing two substances makes tiny gas bubbles?

These are the types of questions that science answers. Science explains what happens when you plant a seed. It explains why popcorn pops. Soon, you will be able to explain things like this too.

The simple, fun experiments in this book will introduce you to topics like pressure, temperature, and motion. Some activities are simple, and some will take a bit more time. Follow the directions, and you will be on your way to thinking like a scientist in no time!

Work Like a Scientist

Scientists have a special way of working. It is a series of steps called the Scientific Method. Follow these steps to work like a scientist.

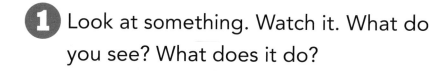

1 Look at something. Watch it. What do you see? What does it do?

2 Think of a question about the thing you are watching. What is it like? Why is it like that? How did it get that way?

3 Try to answer your question.

4 Do a test to find out if you are right. Write down what happened.

5 Think about it. Were you right? Why or why not?

Keep Track

Want to be just like a scientist? Scientists keep notes about everything they do. So, get a notebook. When you do an experiment, write down what happens in each step. It's super simple!

9

Key Symbols

In this book you will see some symbols. Here is what they mean.

 Hot. Get help! You will be working with something hot.

 Adult Help. Get help! You will need help from an adult.

 Safety Glasses. Put on your safety glasses!

 Sharp Object. Be careful! You will be working with a sharp object.

What You'll Need

These are some of the things you'll need
to do the experiments in this book.

string

penny

balloons

straight drinking straws

flat head nails

hex nut

clear tape

wooden cooking skewer

birthday candle

measuring cups

aluminum foil

mugs

matches

books

safety glasses

duct tape

baking dish

wool sweater

chairs

corrugated cardboard

sugar

white vinegar

measuring cup

food coloring

Alka-Seltzer tablet

unpopped popcorn kernels

bowls

utility knife

raisins

eyedropper

yeast

clear plastic cups

hot glue gun

vegetable oil

hydrogen peroxide

gallon plastic jug

empty plastic bottles

funnel

dish soap

measuring spoons

dishwashing detergent

baking soda

wax paper

club soda

green bean seeds

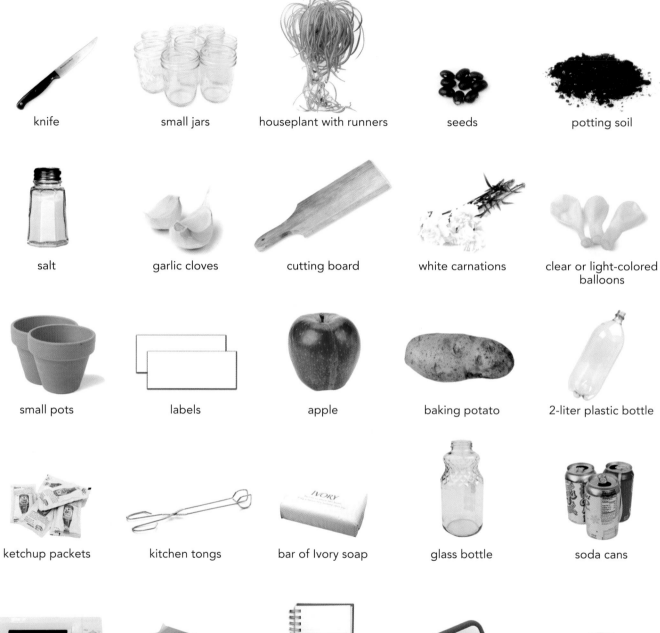

knife

small jars

houseplant with runners

seeds

potting soil

salt

garlic cloves

cutting board

white carnations

clear or light-colored
balloons

small pots

labels

apple

baking potato

2-liter plastic bottle

ketchup packets

kitchen tongs

bar of Ivory soap

glass bottle

soda cans

microwave oven

microwave popcorn

paper

timer

stopper

index card

rubber bands

large paper clip

wool sock

timer

plastic wrap

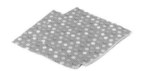

paper napkin

cotton cloth

plastic container with lid

thermometers

pitcher

shoebox

small saucepan

hair dryer

1-liter plastic bottle and cap

handkerchief

flexible tube

large stones

small stones

clear straw

wooden matchsticks

ground pepper

large screw

tall glasses

scissors

That's Repulsive!

Can you keep two balloons from touching each other?

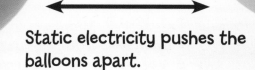

Static electricity pushes the balloons apart.

1. Cut two pieces of string about 30 inches (76 cm) long.

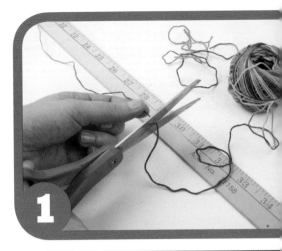

2. Tape one end of each string to the top of a door frame. They should be about 1 inch (2.5 cm) apart.

3. Blow up two balloons and tie them closed. Tie a piece of string to each balloon. The balloons should hang at the same level.

4. Rub each balloon on the wool sweater.

5. Let the balloons go. What happens? What happens if you move the balloons toward each other?

6. Put your hand between the balloons. Now what happens?

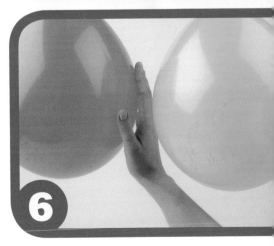

What's Going On?

Rubbing the balloons on wool gives them **static electricity**. This makes them move away from each other. When you put your hand between the balloons, they move toward it. That's because your hand doesn't have static electricity.

Let's Go Nuts!

How can you use a balloon to drive everyone nuts?

The nut makes noise inside the balloon.

1. Put on your safety glasses. Your balloon will **probably** burst at some point.

2. Put a hex nut in a balloon. Blow up the balloon almost all the way. Tie it closed.

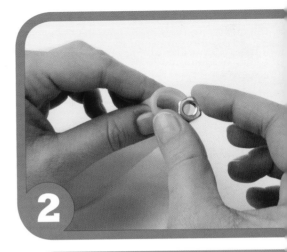

3. **Grab** the top of the balloon with your whole hand. **Swirl** the balloon.

4. Keep swirling until the hex nut circles inside of the balloon. Use your fingertips to hold the bottom of the balloon.

5. What do you see? What do you hear?

6. **Repeat** steps 2 through 4. But this time use a penny instead of a hex nut. Now what do you hear?

What's Going On?

A hex nut has corners. When you swirl the balloon, the corners rub against the balloon. That makes a loud sound. A penny is round and smooth. It doesn't make as much noise.

A Moving Experience

Can you move a mug using only a balloon?

The balloon gets wedged into the mug.

The mug is lifted up.

1. Blow up the balloon part way. It should be a little bigger than the opening of the mug. Do not tie it closed.

2. Hold the balloon closed. Place it on the mug.

3. Blow up the balloon some more. Now tie it closed.

4. Lift up the balloon. What happens?

What's Going On?

A balloon's surface is rubbery. Adding air with the balloon on the mug **wedges** the balloon in. The rubbery surface of the balloon sticks to the mug. It's like it's holding onto the mug!

 PHYSICS

Jet Balloon

Why does a balloon fly like a rocket?

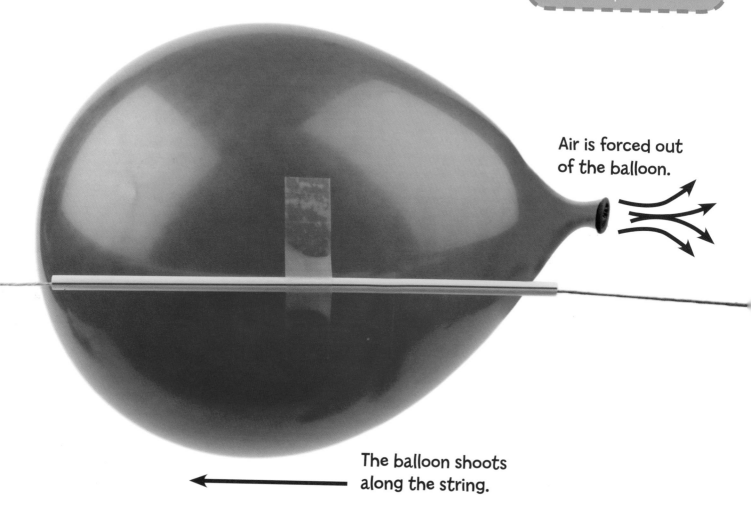

Air is forced out of the balloon.

The balloon shoots along the string.

1. Put the chairs 10 feet (3 m) apart. Tie one end of the string to one chair.

2. Thread the string through the straw. Tie the other end of the string to the other chair. Make sure the string is tight.

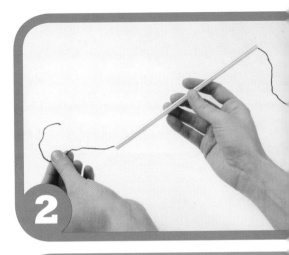

3. Blow up a balloon but don't tie it. Hold the end closed while you do the next step.

4. Move the straw to one end of the string. Tape the balloon to the straw. The opening should point to the closest chair.

5. Let go of the balloon. What happens?

6. **Repeat** steps 3 through 5. Blow the balloon up more or less than the first time. Or use a larger or smaller balloon. What happens this time? Why do you think that is?

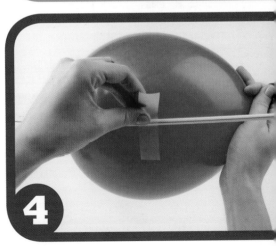

What's Going On?

When you blow up a balloon, it **stretches**. When you let go, the balloon quickly returns to its original size. All the air gets forced out of the opening. This makes the balloon shoot in the direction opposite of the opening.

Stick It to It!

If you poke a balloon with a sharp stick, it will pop, right?

What You'll Need
- safety glasses
- balloon
- wooden cooking skewer
- clear tape

The tape keeps the hole from getting too big.

The skewer doesn't pop the balloon.

1. Put on your safety glasses.

2. Blow up a balloon. Tie it closed.

3. Put a piece of tape on the balloon.

4. Gently push the sharp end of the skewer into the balloon through the tape.

5. Keep pushing the skewer into the balloon. What happens?

What's Going On?

Without the tape, the edges of the hole would pull away from the skewer. That would make the hole bigger and the balloon would pop. The tape keeps the hole the same size as the skewer. The skewer keeps the air in and the balloon doesn't pop.

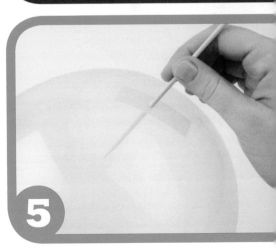

Way Cool Water Balloon

Is a candle too hot to handle?

What You'll Need
- safety glasses
- 2 balloons
- small piece of aluminum foil
- birthday candle
- matches
- measuring cup
- water
- baking dish

Water keeps the balloon cool.

Part 1

1. Put on your safety glasses. Blow up one balloon. Tie it closed.

2. Press the foil around the bottom of the candle so it stands up. Have your adult helper light the candle.

3. Hold the balloon over the flame. What happens?

Part 2

4. Put about ½ cup (118 ml) of water in the other balloon. Blow up the balloon and tie it closed.

5. Put the candle in the baking dish. Hold the balloon over it. What happens this time?

What's Going On?

A balloon with just air pops right away when it touches the flame. That's because all the heat is in one spot. If the balloon has water inside, it doesn't pop right away. The water spreads the heat over a larger area. The balloon stays cool.

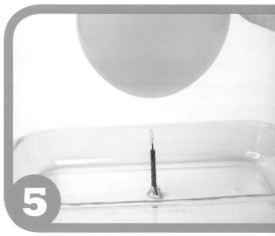

Bed of Nails

How many nails make the balloon fail?

The book makes the pressure even.

No single spot on the balloon gets poked very hard.

Part 1: Make the bed of nails

1 Use the ruler to draw a **grid** on one piece of cardboard. The grid should have 10 lines in each direction. The lines should be ½ inch (1.3 cm) apart.

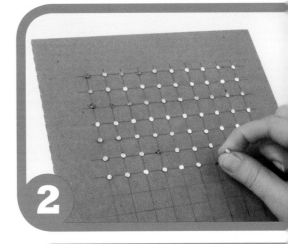

2 Have an adult helper do this step. Poke the nails through the cardboard where the grid lines meet. There should be 10 rows of 10 nails.

3 Carefully set the cardboard down. Put strips of tape over the nail heads. This will hold them in place.

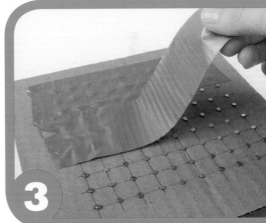

4 Tape the second piece of cardboard on top of the nail heads. Turn the whole thing over so that the nails point up. This is the bed of nails.

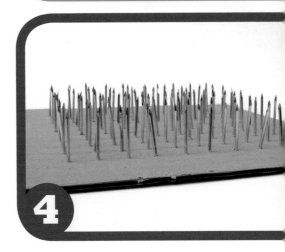

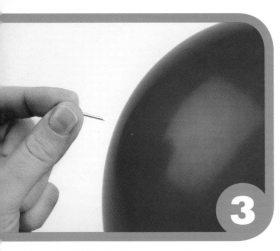

Part 2: Test the balloons

1. Put on your safety glasses.

2. Blow up one balloon and tie it closed.

3. Take the extra nail. Poke the balloon with it. What happens?

4. Blow up another balloon and tie it closed.

5. Carefully lay it on the bed of nails. Does anything happen?

6. Put the book on top of the balloon. Press down gently. What happens?

7. Keep pressing on the balloon. What happens?

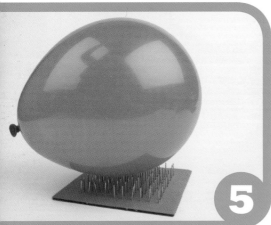

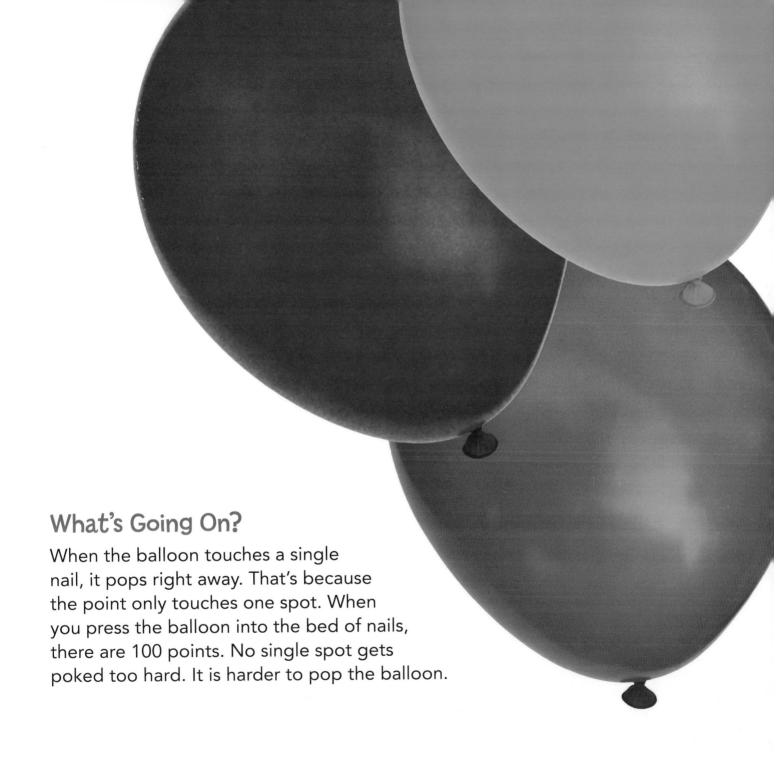

What's Going On?

When the balloon touches a single
nail, it pops right away. That's because
the point only touches one spot. When
you press the balloon into the bed of nails,
there are 100 points. No single spot gets
poked too hard. It is harder to pop the balloon.

 CHEMISTRY

Hip to Be Square

Is a square bubble cooler than a round one?

What You'll Need
- hot glue gun
- wax paper
- 6 straight drinking straws, cut into 12 3½-inch (9 cm) pieces
- scissors
- gallon plastic jug, rinsed
- utility knife
- warm water
- measuring cup
- dish soap (regular not antibacterial)
- glass eyedropper

The soapy water sticks to the bubble frame. That makes a square bubble!

30

Part 1

1 Protect your work surface with a piece of wax paper. Use the hot glue gun to make a square out of four straw pieces. Make another square with four more straw pieces.

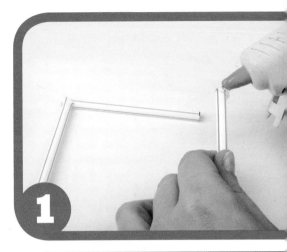

2 Use the remaining four straw pieces to join the two squares. Glue one end of each straw to a corner of one of the squares. The straw pieces should stick up.

3 Glue the corners of the other square to the other ends of the straws. Wait for the glue to dry. Then use scissors to cut off any extra glue. This is the bubble frame.

4 Have your adult helper cut off the top of the plastic jug.

5 Fill the plastic jug almost full with warm water. Add 1 cup (240 ml) of dish soap. Mix it gently with your hand.

Part 2

1. Lower the bubble frame into the soap **mixture**. Push it down until it's completely covered.

2. Slowly pull the frame back out. How does it look?

3. Now, shake it gently. What happens?

4. Pull the rubber top off the eyedropper.

5 Dip the wide end of the dropper into the soap **mixture**. Gently blow through the small end to make a bubble.

6 Dunk the bubble frame again. Drop the round bubble into the top of the bubble frame. The round bubble should fall into the center of the square bubble. How does it look?

What's Going On?

Soap is **stretchy**. It sticks to the surface of water. When you blow into it, it stretches into a bubble. A natural bubble has a round shape. The soapy water also sticks to your bubble frame. That makes a square bubble. When you drop a round bubble onto the square bubble, it falls into the center. That makes a bubble within a bubble!

Popcorn Goes the Raisin

How strong are tiny bubbles?

What You'll Need
- 2 plastic cups of plain water
- 2 plastic cups of club soda
- raisins
- unpopped popcorn kernels

Club soda bubbles lift the raisins and popcorn to the top.

1. Look closely at a raisin and a popcorn kernel. How are they different?

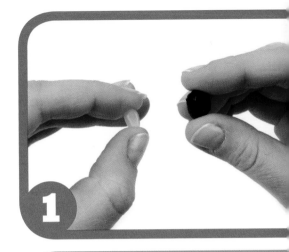

2. Drop three raisins into a cup of plain water. Drop three popcorn kernels into the other cup of plain water. Does anything happen? How about after a few minutes?

3. Drop three raisins into a cup of club soda. Drop three popcorn kernels into the other cup of club soda. What happens this time?

4. Keep watching the cups for a while. What do you observe?

What's Going On?

Bubbles form on the popcorn and raisins in both kinds of water. The bubbles in the plain water are very tiny. The bubbles in the club soda have carbon dioxide gas in them. They get larger. They make the popcorn kernels and raisins float. The bubbles pop. The raisins and kernels fall back to the bottom until new bubbles form.

The wrinkled raisins hold more bubbles than the smooth popcorn. So they rise to the surface faster.

Elephant's Toothpaste

Do you need to squeeze this bottle?

Yeast and hydrogen peroxide make a gas that creates bubbles.

What You'll Need
- measuring spoons
- measuring cups
- yeast
- water
- empty 16-ounce plastic bottle
- hydrogen peroxide
- dish soap (regular not antibacterial)
- food coloring
- funnel
- baking pan

Safety note
The bubbles look like toothpaste, but they are not safe to eat. Do not put them in your mouth! However, it is safe to touch the bubbles.

1. Put 1 teaspoon (5 ml) yeast and 2 tablespoons (30 ml) water in a small measuring cup. Stir until the yeast is **dissolved**.

2. Have an adult helper measure ½ cup (118 ml) hydrogen peroxide. Add three or four drops of food coloring.

3. Stand the plastic bottle in the pan. Put the funnel in the top of the bottle. Pour the hydrogen peroxide **mixture** through the funnel.

4. Put a little dish soap in the bottle.

5. Pour the dissolved yeast into the bottle.

6. What happens? Touch the side of the bottle. How does it feel?

What's Going On?

Mixing yeast with the hydrogen peroxide causes a **chemical reaction**. The mixture makes a gas and bubbles up. It also gets warm. The bubbles look like toothpaste when they come out of the bottle.

That's Lava-ly!

Oil and water don't mix, but will they go with the flow?

The water and food coloring sink below the oil.

The Alka-Seltzer bubbles float up through the oil.

1 Fill the bottle three-quarters full with vegetable oil. Add water until the bottle is full.

2 Add ten drops of food coloring to the bottle.

3 Break the Alka-Seltzer tablet into eight pieces. Drop them into the bottle one at a time. Wait until the bubbling stops before you add the next one. What happens?

4 When the bubbling from the last piece stops, screw on the bottle cap. Tip the bottle back and forth. What does the **mixture** inside look like?

What's Going On?

Oil and water don't mix. The water sinks below the oil. So does the food coloring. When Alka-Seltzer **dissolves** in water, it makes tiny bubbles. The bubbles make the colored water float to the surface. At the surface, the bubbles pop. The colored water falls back to the bottom.

Soap du Jour

Can you turn soap into salt?

What You'll Need
- bowl
- spoon
- powdered laundry or dishwasher detergent
- white vinegar

Carbon dioxide is released and salt remains.

40

1. Put 3 spoonfuls of powdered detergent in the bowl.

2. Add 1 spoonful of white vinegar.

3. **Swirl** the bowl to mix well. What happens?

What's Going On?

Mixing vinegar and soap causes a **chemical reaction**. That means the vinegar and soap combine and turn into other things. Bubbles of carbon dioxide are released from the **mixture**. A kind of salt is left behind.

Safety note
The salt left behind when the gas bubbles away is not safe to eat. Do not put it in your mouth!

It's a Gas, Gas, Gas!

How many ways can you blow up a balloon?

What You'll Need
- 2 balloons
- measuring spoons
- measuring cup
- hot water
- 1 packet yeast
- sugar
- 2 empty 16-ounce plastic bottles
- funnel
- baking soda
- white vinegar

The yeast eats the sugar and releases gas bubbles. The bubbles fill the balloon.

The vinegar and baking soda cause a chemical reaction. Gas bubbles from the reaction fill the balloon.

Part 1

1 Blow up the balloons and let out the air. Do this to each balloon four or five times. This will **stretch** them out a little.

2 Put the yeast and 2 tablespoons (30 ml) of sugar in the measuring cup. Add enough hot water to make 1 cup (237 ml). Let the **mixture** sit for 2 minutes.

3 Pour the yeast mixture into one of the plastic bottles.

4 Quickly stretch one balloon over the top of the bottle. Check it every 30 minutes. What happens?

Part 2

1 Pour 1 tablespoon (15 ml) of vinegar into the second plastic bottle.

2 Put the funnel in the other balloon. Pour 1 teaspoon (5 ml) of baking soda through the funnel.

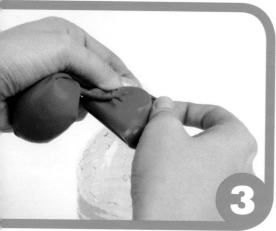

3 Twist the top of the balloon closed. Hold it closed while you **stretch** the mouth of the balloon over the mouth of the bottle.

4 Hold the balloon straight up. Untwist it so that the baking soda falls into the vinegar in the bottle. What happens? How does it compare with the yeast bottle?

What's Going On?

Yeast is a living **organism**. When you add warm water, the yeast feeds on the sugar. The yeast releases bubbles of gas as a result of eating. The gas slowly builds up inside the bottle. Then it starts filling the balloon.

Mixing baking soda and vinegar also produces gas bubbles. These bubbles are the result of a **chemical reaction**. They fill their bottle and blow up the balloon. They do it much faster than the yeast's gas bubbles.

Bean There, Done That!

Can you make a bean sprout?

Sprouts and roots grow out of the seed.

Sprouts grow up.

Roots grow down.

1. Fill the cup with potting soil. Use your finger to poke three holes in the soil. The holes should be about 2 inches (5 cm) deep. Make them along the sides of the cup. That way you can see your seeds **sprout**!

2. Drop one seed into each hole. Fill in the holes.

3. Water the seeds. Put the cup in a warm spot with a lot of light.

4. Water the seeds again when the soil is dry. Look at them every day. What do you see? How do the seeds change?

What's Going On?

Planting a seed is one way to start a new plant. The seed sends roots down into the soil. A sprout grows up toward the light.

New Plant in Town!

Do you always need a seed to grow a new plant?

The plantlet grows roots when left in water.

Before

After

1. Fill the jar about halfway with water.

2. The small plants at the end of the runners on the spider plant are called plantlets. Cut off one plantlet.

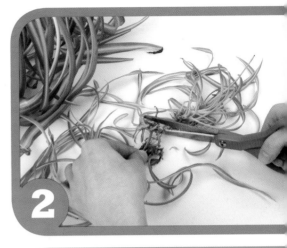

3. Put the bottom of the plantlet in the water.

4. Put the jar on a windowsill. Wait two or three weeks. Look at it every day. Make sure the bottom of the plantlet stays underwater. What happens?

5. Plant your plantlet in potting soil. Water it. Now you have a new plant!

What's Going On?

Many kinds houseplants send out runners with plantlets on the ends. When you put a plantlet in water, roots grow from the bottom. Then you can plant it in a pot of dirt. It will keep growing. You don't even need a seed!

Get to the Point

Does it matter which way the point points?

Point Up

The shoot still grows up.

Roots still grow down.

Point Down

1. Fill each cup with soil. Poke a hole in the dirt of each cup. Make them along the sides of the cups.

2. Put a **garlic** clove in each hole. In one cup, the clove's point should point up. In the other cup, it should point down.

3. Label the cups POINT UP and POINT DOWN. Cover the cloves with soil.

4. Water both cups. Put them in a bright place. Water the cloves again when the soil is dry.

5. What happens? Does the **sprout** appear at the same time in both cups?

What's Going On?

A garlic clove is a kind of seed called a bulb. A new plant starts from a bulb. The bulb sends a sprout from the pointed end up toward the light. Roots grow down into the soil from the flat end. When the pointed end is down, a sprout still grows up from it. But it takes longer to come out of the dirt.

 BIOLOGY

Seed What Happens

How important are light and water to a plant?

The watered seeds sprout.

The dry seeds do nothing.

1. Fill each pot with soil.

2. Poke a hole in the soil in each pot.

3. Drop a few seeds in each hole. Cover the seeds with soil.

4. Water one of the pots. Do not water the other pot. Put both pots in a bright place.

5. Check the pots every day. If the soil in the pot that you watered feels dry, add a little water. Do not water the other pot.

6. What happens? Do the seeds in both pots grow?

What's Going On?

Plants and seeds need light and water to grow. The seeds that you watered **sprouted** after a few days. The seeds in the other pot did not.

Balloon Botany

Are balloons good for more than birthday parties?

What You'll Need
- clear or light-colored balloon
- funnel
- measuring cup
- potting soil
- tablespoon
- water
- seeds
- string

The ballon holds in water.

The seeds grow.

54

1. Blow up the balloon and then let the air out. Do this a few times to **stretch** the balloon.

2. Using the funnel, put ½ cup (118 ml) of soil into the balloon. Pour 4 tablespoons (59 ml) of water into the balloon.

3. Drop a few seeds into the balloon.

4. Blow up the balloon. Tie it closed.

5. Tap the side of the balloon a few times. The soil, water, and seeds should fall to the bottom.

6. Hang the balloon in front of a window. What happens?

What's Going On?

The balloon acts like a greenhouse. It is tied closed so no air can get in. That keeps the water from drying up. It keeps itself watered. The seeds **sprout** just like they would in a pot.

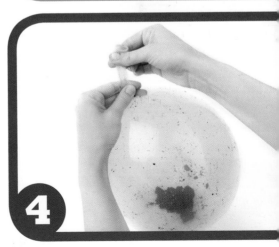

Shrink and Shrivel

How much water is in a plant?

The salt mixture draws even more water out. This piece is smaller.

The air draws a lot of water out of the apple.

Both pieces shrink and shrivel.

1. Have your adult helper cut the apple into four pieces. Put one piece into each of the cups. Eat the other two pieces for a healthy snack.

2. Mix together ²/₃ cup (158 ml) salt and ¹/₃ cup (79 ml) baking soda.

3. Pour the salt **mixture** into one of the cups. Make sure the apple is **completely** covered. Leave the other apple piece by itself in the other cup.

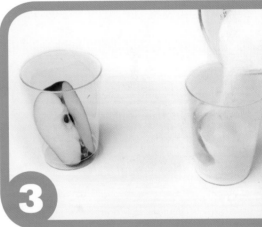

4. Let the two cups sit in a dark place for one week. Then take the apple piece out of the salt mixture. Brush it off, but don't rinse it in water. Compare it with the plain apple piece. How do the two pieces look?

What's Going On?

Plants contain a lot of water. The air dries some of the water out of the first apple piece. That causes it to shrivel. The salt mixture pulls even more water out of the other apple piece. That piece becomes smaller than the piece that dried in the air. The water from the apple piece makes the salt mixture stick together.

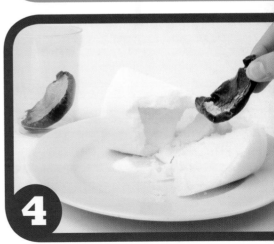

Carnation Caper

Can you change the color of a flower?

The carnations "drink" the colored water.
They turn the same color as the water.

58

Part 1

1 Fill four jars about half full with water.

2 Add 25 drops of food coloring to each jar. Use a different color in each one.

3 Have your adult helper cut the stems of four flowers. Make the stems about twice as tall as the jars.

4 Put one flower into each jar. Each carnation will drink one color of water. What do you think will happen?

Part 2

1 Do steps 1 and 2 from Part 1 using the other four jars.

2 Have an adult cut the stems of the last two carnations lengthwise. The cuts should be a little longer than the jars are tall.

3 Place two jars of water next to each other. Put one half of a flower stem in each jar.

4 Do the same for the second carnation and the other two jars.

5 Each of these carnations will drink two colors of water. What do you think will happen this time?

Part 3

1 Check all the carnations every few hours. What is happening? How do the carnations that drink one color of water look? How do the carnations that drink two colors of water look? Is there a difference? Do the flowers drink the different colors at the same speed?

What's Going On?

A plant draws water up its stem. It's like what happens when you drink through a straw. The carnation sucks the colored water all the way up to the top. It changes the color of the flower.

CHEMISTRY

Pop the Stopper

What does it take to pop the stopper?

What You'll Need
- safety glasses
- empty 2-liter bottle
- stopper that fits the bottle
- vinegar
- measuring cup
- measuring spoon
- baking soda

pop

Gas builds up.

62

1. Put on your safety glasses.

2. Pour ½ cup (118 ml) vinegar into the bottle.

3. Put 2 teaspoons (10 ml) of baking soda into the bottle. Hold the bottle away from you. Quickly put the stopper in. Do not use the screw-on cap.

4. Point the top of the bottle away from yourself and anyone else in the room. Shake the bottle. Wait a few seconds. What happens?

5. Rinse the bottle. Do steps 1 through 4 again. Use a little more or less vinegar or baking soda. Does this affect the result? If so, how?

What's Going On?

When you mix vinegar and baking soda, it makes a gas. The gas fills up the bottle. When there is no more room, pressure from the gas pushes the stopper out of the bottle.

Don't Mess with Ketchup

Why does a ketchup packet explode when you step on it?

Stomp on it.

1. Go outside.

2. Lay a ketchup **packet** flat on the ground.

3. **Stomp** on it! Aim for one side of the packet. What happens?

4. Use paper towels to clean up. Clean the sidewalk and your shoe!

What's Going On?

Stomping on the packet makes less space inside it. The ketchup can't fit inside anymore. So it bursts through the packet!

Potato Plunger

How can an ordinary plastic straw pierce a potato?

The straw goes through it.

1. Hold the potato firmly in one hand. Make sure to hold the potato near the end.

2. Pick up a straw with your other hand. **Stab** the potato hard with the straw. What happens?

3. Take another straw. This time put your thumb over the top of the straw.

4. Stab the potato again. What happens this time?

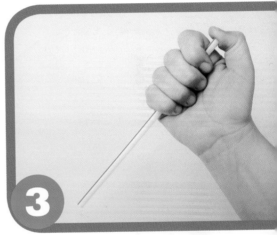

What's Going On?

A soft plastic straw is no match for a potato. Putting your thumb over one end traps air in the straw. The air pressure in the straw increases when the straw hits the potato. Air presses against the sides of the straw. That makes the straw stiff. The straw goes right through the potato.

Crush the Can

Can you crush a soda can without stepping on it?

The sides of the can get pushed in.

68

1 Put on your safety glasses. Fill the bowl halfway with cold water.

2 Put 2 tablespoons (30 ml) of water into an empty soda can.

3 Set the soda can on a stove **burner**. Have your adult helper turn on the burner.

4 Wait until the water in the can bubbles. That means it is boiling. Wait one more minute.

5 Hold the tongs with your palm up. Pick up the soda can with the tongs.

6 Quickly flip the can over and stick the open end into the water. Hold it there. What happens?

What's Going On?

As the water boils, it turns into water vapor. The vapor pushes air out of the can. When you put the can into cold water, the vapor quickly cools. It turns back into water. That leaves extra room. Air can't fill the space because the can's **opening** is underwater. Pressure from the air outside pushes the sides of the can in.

 CHEMISTRY

Balloon vs. Bottle

Will a balloon go into a
bottle without bursting?

What You'll Need
- balloons
- glass bottle with a
  wide mouth, such
  as a juice bottle
  (rinsed out and
  clean)
- water
- strips of paper
- matches
- drinking straw

The balloon gets pulled in.

The paper burns.

70

Part 1: Balloon In

1 Make a water balloon. It should be a little bigger than the mouth of the bottle. Tie it shut.

2 Rub some water around the mouth of the bottle.

3 Have your adult helper do this step. Light a match. Set one strip of paper on fire. Put the burning strip into the bottle.

4 You can do this step. Set the water balloon on top of the bottle. What happens to the fire? What does the balloon do?

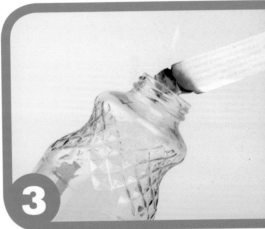

What's Going On?

The burning paper made the air inside the bottle warm. Warm air takes up more room than cool air. When you put the balloon on top of the bottle, the fire goes out. The air cools down and takes up less room. That makes more space inside the bottle. The pressure of the air from outside pushes the balloon into the bottle.

Part 2: Balloon Out

1 Rub water around the mouth of the bottle again.

2 Try pulling the balloon out. Are you able to?

3 Now put a straw in the bottle.

4 Try pulling the balloon out again. What happens this time?

What's Going On?

The first time, the balloon gets caught in the mouth of the bottle. That's because no air can get around it. When you add the straw, it lets air into the bottle. The air pressure inside and outside the bottle stays equal. That lets you pull the balloon out of the bottle.

Microwave Magic

Can a microwave oven help you with science?

The air or water inside gets bigger and the stuff gets puffy.

Part 1: Billowing Soap

1 Unwrap the bar of Ivory soap. Break it in half.

2 Lay a paper towel in the microwave. Put one half of the soap in the center.

3 Set the oven to high. Cook the soap for 90 seconds. Watch it carefully. What happens?

4 Safety first! It is important to let the soap cool for a couple of minutes. Then take it out of the microwave. What does it look like? How does it feel?

What's Going On?

A lot of air is trapped inside Ivory soap. Cooking the soap in the microwave warms and **softens** it. The air trapped inside the soap also gets warm. It starts to get bigger. The pressure of the air causes the soap to form a light and **puffy** shape.

Part 2: Popcorn Puzzle

1 Look closely at a few unpopped popcorn **kernels**. How do they look? How do they feel?

2 Prepare the microwave popcorn. Follow the directions on the label.

3 Remove the bag of popped corn from the microwave. Point it away from your face. Pull it open.

4 Pour the popcorn into a bowl. Now how does it look and feel? Enjoy a yummy snack!

What's Going On?

A popcorn kernel has a little bit of water in it. Cooking popcorn turns the water inside each kernel into steam. Steam takes up more room than water. The pressure of the steam causes the kernel to explode! That's what makes the **puffy** treat that we love to eat.

Hot and Cold

What effect does temperature have on water?

What You'll Need

- plastic container with lid
- water
- freezer
- measuring cup
- small saucepan
- stove

Heating makes the water turn into steam.

Freezing causes water to **expand**.

76

Part 1: Hot

1 Measure ½ cup (118 ml) of water. Pour it into the saucepan. Place the pan on the stove.

2 Have your adult helper heat the water until it boils. You will know it is boiling when it bubbles.

3 Watch the water closely for a few minutes. Be careful not to get your face in the steam. What do you observe?

What's Going On?

When water boils, it turns into steam. Steam is a gas. The steam rises into the air. Don't let it boil too long. After a while all of the water will be gone!

Part 2: Cold

1 Fill the plastic container with water. Lay the cover over the top, but don't seal it.

2 Put the container in the freezer. Leave it there overnight.

3 Remove the container from the freezer. How does it look?

What's Going On?

Water **expands** when it freezes. The ice becomes bigger than the container. It pushes the cover up. If you let the ice thaw, the water will fit in the container again.

Insulation Fascination

How can you keep your hots hotter and your colds colder?

Some **materials** are better than others at keeping the **temperature** from changing.

Part 1

1 Line up the mugs. Have an adult help with the next step. Pour the same amount of very hot water into each mug. Be careful not to splash hot water on yourself.

2 Cover one mug each with the sock, cotton cloth, foil, and paper napkin. Use rubber bands to hold the covers in place.

3 Wait 45 minutes.

4 Take the covers off the mugs.

5 Put a **thermometer** in each mug. Which one is still the warmest?

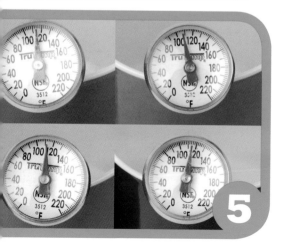

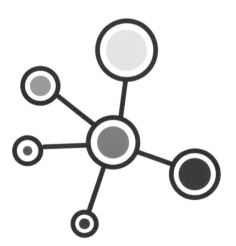

Part 2

1 This time, pour cold water into each mug.

2 Cover one mug each with the sock, cotton cloth, foil, and paper napkin. Use rubber bands to hold the covers in place.

3 Wait 45 minutes.

4 Take the covers off the mugs.

5 Put a **thermometer** in each mug. Which one is still the coldest? Did the same **material** work the best for both hot and cold?

What's Going On?

Some things are good at holding in the heat or cold. Some things are not. What the material is made of makes a difference. The thickness of the material is also important.

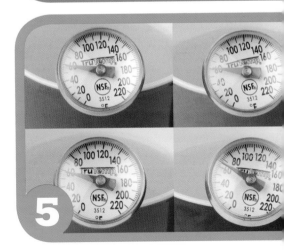

Heat by the Numbers

Why do animals and insects huddle together to stay warm?

A single jar cools off faster than a group of jars.

Part 1

1 Have your adult helper heat the water on the stove. When it begins to steam, have your helper fill one jar.

2 Cover the jar with plastic wrap. Poke a **thermometer** through the plastic wrap.

3 Wait for the **temperature** to stop rising. Record the temperature.

4 Wait 30 minutes. Record the temperature again.

5 Empty the jar.

Part 2

1 Group four jars so that they touch.

2 Have your adult helper reheat the water. When it begins to steam, have your helper fill all four jars.

3 Cover the jars with plastic wrap. Poke the **thermometers** through the plastic wrap. Make sure the jars are still touching.

4 Wait for the **temperatures** to be about the same as the first temperature in Part 1. Start the timer.

5 Wait 30 minutes. Record the temperatures. Are they higher or lower than in Part 1?

6 Wait until the temperatures are about the same as the second temperature in Part 1. How long did it take?

What's Going On?

The single jar loses heat from all sides. So it cools faster than the jars in a group. The grouped jars only lose heat from the outsides. So they cool more slowly.

Stretch It Out

How does temperature affect the stretch of a rubber band?

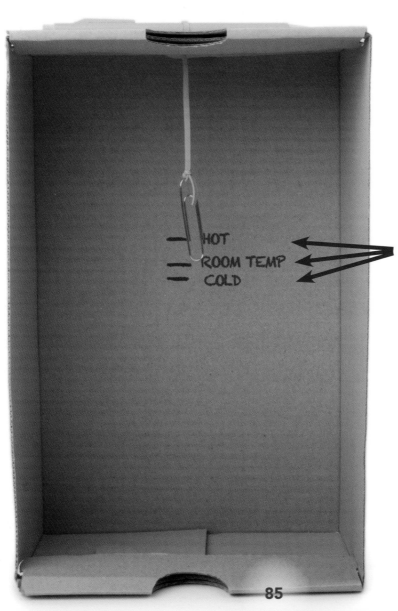

A rubber band changes length when it is heated or cooled.

HOT
ROOM TEMP
COLD

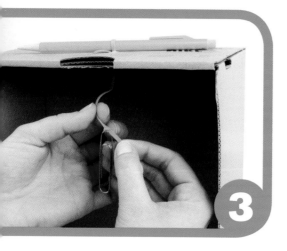

1 Cut the rubber band once. Tie one end around the pencil.

2 Stand the shoebox on a short side. Poke a hole in the top of the shoebox. Thread the loose end of the rubber band through it. Rest the pencil on the outside of the box.

3 Tie the loose end of the rubber band around the paper clip. Let the paper clip hang for a few minutes. If it touches the bottom, use a shorter rubber band.

4 On the inside of the box, mark how far down it hangs.

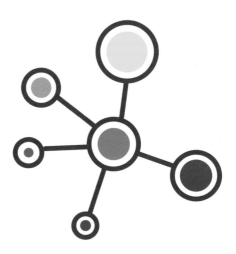

5 Put the shoebox in the refrigerator. After 20 minutes, open the door. Mark how far down the paper clip hangs after cooling. Then take the box out of the refrigerator.

6 Use the hair dryer to heat the rubber band for 5 minutes. Mark how far down the paper clip hangs after heating.

7 Compare all of the marks. Are you surprised by the results?

What's Going On?

Most **substances** get larger when they are heated. And they get smaller when they are cooled.
A rubber band does the opposite. It gets longer when you cool it. It gets shorter when you heat it.

Purple Passion

Everyone knows that blue and red make purple, right?

Hot and cold water don't mix.

1. Place one jar in the baking pan. Fill it part way with very cold water. Stir in one drop of blue food coloring. Add more cold water until the jar is **completely** full.

2. Pour very hot water into the other jar. Stir in one drop of red food coloring. Add more hot water until the jar is completely full.

3. Place the index card over the top of the red jar. Press it down gently.

4. Keep pressing the index card and quickly turn the jar over. The index card will hold the water in. Set the upside-down jar on top of the blue jar. Line up the jar rims.

5. Have a helper hold onto both jars. Carefully pull the index card out from between them. What happens?

What's Going On?

The cold and hot water don't mix. That's because cold water has a higher **density** than hot water. It stays on the bottom. Hot water has a lower density than cold water. It stays on the top.

Top and Bottom

Oil floats on water, right?

What You'll Need
- small, clear jar or glass
- vegetable oil
- water
- ice cube

The ice cube floats in oil.

The oil floats on water.

1. Fill the jar half full with vegetable oil.

2. Pour some water into the jar. What happens?

3. Now add the ice cube. What happens this time?

What's Going On?

Oil has a lower **density** than liquid water. So it floats on top of the water. But when water freezes into ice, it **expands** and its density increases. So the ice cube floats in the oil.

Bottled Up

Water will leak out
of a hole, right?

Removing the cap
allows water to
leak out the hole.

1. Poke a hole near the bottom of the bottle with the screw.

2. Hold your finger over the hole. Fill the bottle with water. Screw on the cap.

3. Hold the bottle over the baking dish. Slowly remove your finger from the hole. Try not to **squeeze** the bottle with your other hand. Does anything happen?

4. Unscrew the cap. What happens now?

What's Going On?

When the cap is on the bottle, air pressure can't push down on the water inside the bottle. So the water does not **leak** out. But when you unscrew the cap, air pushes into the bottle. The water streams out of the hole.

Super Simple Siphon

Can you move water from one glass to another without pouring?

Water flows through the tube until the level is the same in both glasses.

1. Fill both glasses half full with water. Put one end of the tube into one of the glasses.

2. Suck on the other end of the tube just until the water fills the tube.

3. Remove the tube from your mouth, quickly putting your finger over the end. There should be little or no air in the tube. Put the covered end into the other glass of water. Remove your finger.

4. Place one glass on the pile of books. What happens to the water level?

5. **Switch** the glasses. Now what happens?

What's Going On?

Air pressure pushes down on the water. That causes water from the upper glass to flow into the lower glass until the levels are even. When you switch the two glasses, the levels even out again.

Pack It In

Do small and large stones take up the same amount of space?

There is less empty space between the small stones.

There is more empty space between the stones.

96

1. Fill one glass with small stones. Fill the other glass with large stones. Fill both glasses to the top with water.

2. Pour the water from the glass of large stones into the measuring cup. Hold the stones in the glass with your fingers. Write down how much water you poured out.

3. Empty the measuring cup. Pour the water from the glass of small stones into the measuring cup. Write down how much water you poured out of the glass.

4. Are the two amounts of water the same? Are they different? Why do you think this is?

What's Going On?

The glass with large stones holds a little more water than the glass with small stones. That's because there is more room between the stones. The small stones are packed more tightly. There is less room in between for water.

Expand Your Horizon

Can a drop of soap push pepper and move matches?

What You'll Need
- baking pan
- water
- ground pepper
- liquid dish soap
- wooden matchsticks

The soap spreads out on the water. It pushes the pepper and matches away.

Part 1

1 Fill the baking pan with water about 1 inch (2.5 cm) deep.

2 Sprinkle several shakes of pepper into the water.

3 Put one drop of dish soap in the middle of the pepper.

4 What happens?

Part 2

1 Empty and rinse the baking pan. Fill it again with 1 inch (2.5 cm) of water.

2 Put 40 wooden matchsticks in the water. They can touch, but they should not be on top of each other.

3 Put one drop of dish soap into the middle of the matchsticks.

4 What happens?

What's Going On?

The pepper sits on the surface of the water. When a drop of soap hits the water, a thin **layer** of soap spreads out over the surface of the water. The soap pushes the pepper away. The same thing happens with the matchsticks, even though they are bigger.

Sealed Up Tight

How many ways can you hold water in?

What You'll Need
- pitcher
- tall glass
- cotton cloth
- water
- wide-mouthed jar
- index card that is wider than the mouth of the jar
- baking pan

Thin layers of water on the card and cloth keep water from spilling.

101

Part 1

1 Put the cloth over the glass. Use your finger to push it into the glass. Fill the glass most of the way with water.

2 Slowly pull the cloth down the outside of the glass. Pull until it is tight across the top of the glass.

3 Put one hand over the top of the glass. Turn the glass over with your other hand. Hold it over the baking pan, just in case.

4 Slowly move your hand away from the glass. What happens?

Part 2

1 Fill the jar with water all the way to the top.

2 Put the index card over the mouth of the jar. Hold it there as you turn the jar upside down.

3 Hold the jar over the cake pan, just in case. Remove the hand that's holding the index card. What happens?

4 Try shaking the jar gently. Does the card stay in place?

What's Going On?

When the cloth gets wet, water clings to small spaces between threads. This creates a thin **layer** of water on the cloth. It keeps the rest of the water from **leaking** out of the glass. A layer of water also forms on the index card. It holds the card to the jar and keeps the water in.

 PHYSICS

Straw Pole

Do yellow and blue always make green?

Adding salt changes the density of the water. Different colors don't mix.

Part 1

1 Fill each cup with water. Add 10 drops of a different food coloring to each cup.

2 Going from left to right, add salt to each cup. Add 1 teaspoon (5 ml) to the first cup. Add 2 teaspoons (10 ml) to the second cup. Add 3 teaspoons (15 ml) to the third cup. Add 4 teaspoons (20 ml) to the fourth cup.

3 Stir each cup until the salt **dissolves**.

4 Once again, go from left to right. Stick one end of the straw about 1 inch (2.5 cm) into the first cup. Put your finger over the other end of the straw. Take the straw out of the cup. A little water is held inside the straw.

5 Keep your finger over the end of the straw. Hold it straight up and down. Stick it 2 inches (5 cm) into the second cup. Slowly remove your finger from the end. Then put your finger back over the end of the straw.

6 Remove the straw and stick it 3 inches (7.6 cm) into the third cup. Slowly remove your finger. Put your finger back over the end of the straw.

7 Remove the straw and stick it 4 inches (10 cm) into the fourth cup. Slowly remove your finger. Put your finger back over the end of the straw.

8 Pull the straw out. Have the colors mixed? Or are they still separate?

Part 2

1 Fill the two jars almost full with water.

2 Add 10 drops of yellow food coloring to one jar. Add 10 drops of blue food coloring to the other.

3 Add 1 teaspoon (5 ml) of salt to the yellow jar. Add 2 teaspoons (10 ml) of salt to the blue jar. Stir each jar until the salt **dissolves**.

4 Put the jars in the baking pan, just in case. Add more water to the jars so that they are **completely** full.

5 Place the index card over the yellow jar. Hold it there as you turn the jar upside down.

6 Set the yellow jar on top of the blue jar. Keep the index card between them. Line up the jar rims.

7 Have a helper hold the jars. Slowly pull the index card out from between them. What happens?

What's Going On?

When you add salt to water, you increase its **density**. Density affects how much the water floats or sinks. The water that has the least salt floats at the top. The water that has the most salt stays at the bottom.

GLOSSARY

activity – something you do for fun or to learn about something.

burner – a round, flat part of a stove that gets hot.

chemical reaction – when mixing two or more things together causes a change or makes a new substance.

completely – entirely or in every way.

congratulations – something you say to someone who has done well or accomplished something.

density – how heavy something is for its size.

dissolve – to mix with a liquid so that it becomes part of the liquid.

expand – to become larger.

garlic – a plant that grows from a bulb which has a strong smell and taste and is used in cooking.

grab – to take hold of something suddenly.

grid – a pattern with rows of squares, such as a checkerboard.

kernel – a grain or seed of a plant such as corn, wheat, or oats.

layer – one thickness of a material or a substance lying over or under another.

leak – to get in or out of something through a small crack or hole.

material – something that other things can be made of, such as fabric, plastic, or metal.

mixture – a combination of two or more different things.

opening – a hole that something can pass through.

organism – a living thing, such as a plant, animal, or bacteria.

packet – a small and usually flat package.

probably – very likely to happen.

puffy – light and soft looking.

repeat – to do or say something again.

sprout – 1. to begin to grow. 2. a new plant growing from a seed.

squeeze – to press the sides of something together.

stab – to poke something with a sharp object.

static electricity – electricity that is on an object, often created by rubbing the object against something.

stomp – to step on something hard and suddenly.

stretch – to get bigger or longer.

substance – anything that takes up space, such as a solid object or a liquid.

swirl – to whirl or to move smoothly in circles.

switch – to change places or take turns.

temperature – a measure of how hot or cold something is.

thermometer – a tool used to measure temperature.

wedge – to push or squeeze something into a small space.

INDEX